"THE BLUES ARE THE ROOTS;
EVERYTHING ELSE IS THE FRUITS."

WILLIE DIXON

For Marielle, Enzo and Mathéo.

In memory of my grandmother, Dorothy Chase,
for passing down her love for blues and folk
music—and for inviting me to that
unforgettable concert!

A FREEDOM THREE BOOK

Published by Freedom Three Publishing
Text Copyright © 2018 by Joel Harper
Illustrations Copyright © 2018 by Gary Kelley
Book Design by Bryant Hodson

Freedom Three Publishing
310 N. Indian Hill Blvd. #442, Claremont, CA 91711
www.freedomthree.com

ISBN: 978-0-9714254-7-7   Library of Congress Control Number: 2017914014

Printed in the U.S.A. by Worzalla

First Edition 10 9 8 7 6 5 4 3 2 1

Freedom Three Publishing saved the following resources by using Utopia U2:XG paper:

★ TREES SAVED: 8.4 trees

★ ENERGY SAVED: 3.8 million BTU's

★ GREENHOUSE GASES REDUCED: 2586 lbs of CO2

★ WASTEWATER REDUCED: 3927 gal

★ SOLID WASTE REDUCTION: 263 lbs

ENVIRONMENTAL BENEFITS STATEMENT
This book is printed on Appleton Utopia U2:XG Extra Green paper. It is made with 30% PCRF (Post-Consumer Recovered Fiber) and Green Power. It is FSC®-certified, acid free, and ECF (Elemental Chlorine-Free). All of the electricity required to manufacture the paper used to print this book is matched with RECS (Renewable Energy Credits) from Green-e© certified energy sources, primarily wind.

Frankie finds the Blues

STORY
JOEL HARPER

PICTURES
GARY KELLEY

FOREWORD BY
TAJ MAHAL

Throughout my career in music, I have often been asked: "What is the state of blues these days? Can this great American genre survive in modern times with the preponderance of music from computers, drum machines, and auto-tuned vocals? Are young people still interested in learning how to play musical instruments?"

Fortunately, there is a musical revolution going on across this continent and around the globe that is not represented in music or entertainment magazines, television, and popular talent programs. Young people *are* learning to play this music!

For starters, blues (like its close relative jazz) has become a global musical language, with people all over the world playing it. They are making pilgrimages to visit the American South and going to the towns, homes, plantations, and juke joints just to get a feel for the areas where this powerful, emotional music sprang from.

This brings us to *Frankie Finds the Blues*. What a lovely story of a child learning from his grandmother about this great music and the intergenerational communication and exchange of culture. *Frankie* is written with love, beauty, great care, and respect.

A story like this would have meant so much to my young soul back in the early 50's when blues music first struck a chord deep within me. Readers who share this book with their children, grandchildren, and great-grandchildren are passing on a priceless gift to future generations.

TAJ MAHAL

"Hello?"

"Hello, Frankie."

"Hi, grandma! What's up?"

"I have two tickets to a blues concert tonight. Would you like to join me?" asked Frankie's grandmother.

"What kind of music is blues?" asked Frankie. "I like hip hop."

"If you like hip hop, I think you will enjoy the show. Hip hop came from the blues," said his grandmother.

"Really?" replied Frankie. "Sure, let's go!"

"The music is beautiful," Frankie whispered to his grandmother. "It sounds like he is playing *10 guitars* at the same time."

"That is called fingerpicking," she whispered back. "I'll explain it more after the concert."

THE MUSIC MADE FRANKIE FEEL LIKE HE WAS TAKEN ON A JOURNEY.

"Fingerpicking originated from African American blues guitarists in the South over 100 years ago. The thumb holds down the bass notes:

THUMP, THUMP, THUMP!

And the other fingers play the treble notes:

PING, PING, TWANG, PING!

It's not easy to learn, but you can do anything you set your mind to, Frankie," said his grandmother.

"How was the concert?" asked Frankie's mother, as
he dashed through the front door and out the back.

"It was amazing! I have to find my guitar. Isn't it in the garage somewhere? I'm going to learn how to fingerpick and play the blues!"

"And mom, did you know that people in Africa were taken away from their families and brought to the United States? They had to work all day for free. They sang *work songs* to help them feel better which developed into the blues. And that is where hip hop came from! I learned all about it at the concert."

"That's right sweetheart," said Frankie's mother. "Music was the one thing that could not be taken away from them."

He tried to learn to play guitar by listening to the music his grandmother bought him at the concert, but he needed some help.

During Frankie's first lesson, he remembered why he stopped playing the guitar. It was hard work, and *IT HURT HIS FINGERS!*

But

this

time,

he

would

not

give

up.

"Frankie, you always play the same song."
"Can you play Hip Hop on the guitar?"

Frankie dreamed that one day he would learn to play the blues.

Frankie liked to play the guitar in the park across the street from his house.

"Sounding real good," came a voice from just over Frankie's shoulder.

It was the fellow he often saw sleeping on the park benches and collecting cans around the neighborhood.

"Thank you," replied Frankie.
"I'm trying to learn how
to fingerpick and play
the blues. Do you play an
instrument?"

"I played the guitar
growing up."

"Do you know how to play
the blues?"

To Frankie's amazement, he began listening to the most beautiful music.

The park paused to listen:

THUMP, THUMP, THUMP,
PING, PING, PING,
THUMP, THUMP, PING, PING,
THUMP, THUMP.

"Can you teach me how to play like that?"

"As long as it's alright with your parents, I suppose I can try. My name's Walter."

"My name's Frankie. I have to go and do my homework now. See you tomorrow, same time, same place?"

"Same time, same place it is," replied Walter.

"Hey, mom! Guess what? I met a guitar player in the park today. He said he would give me lessons. His name is Walter and he knows how to play the blues!"

"You want to take guitar lessons from a man in the park? You know better than to talk to strangers, Frankie!" said his mother.

"I know, mom! But I see him around town all the time. I think he lives in the park."

"You mean the man with the bedroll on his back, looking for food in garbage cans? He plays the guitar?" replied Frankie's mother.

"Yes, that's him. He's collecting cans, mom! He recycles them for money!"

"He has been in this community for as long as I can remember," said Frankie's grandmother.

The next day after school, Frankie took his mother and grandmother to the park to meet Walter.

"Good day, sir," said Frankie's mother. "My son says that the two of you discussed guitar lessons?"

"Yes, ma'am. Please, call me Walter, Walter Brown. I may be homeless, but I'm harmless."

"I'm not sure how I feel about this," said Frankie's mother.

"But mom, I want to learn how to fingerpick! Walter, please, take my guitar... play a song for them!"

Walter wailed out one beautiful note after another:

"Sittin' here listening to the birds... tryin' not to let life pass me by... Will I make it back to that place I call home..."

His fingers hammered down on the guitar strings:

THUMP, THUMP, PING, PING, PING, THUMP, THUMP.

"Your music sounds wonderful," said Frankie's mother.

"Thank you, ma'am."

"Please, call me Ida, and this is Frankie's grandmother, Marian."

"Where did you learn how to play the guitar?" asked Marian.

"My father taught me how to play when I was about your age, Frankie."

Frankie's mother and grandmother were both won over by Walter's sincerity and his melodic music.

Frankie was so grateful for the guitar lessons that he used money from his own savings and bought Walter a guitar.

They continued to play music together, often attracting crowds of people that would stop to enjoy their music.

"YOU CAN'T JUDGE A BOOK BY LOOKIN' AT THE COVER."

BO DIDDLEY